KINGFISHER READERS

level

1

Tyrannosaurus!

Thea Feldman

KINGFISHER

NEW YORK

KINGFISHER
LONDON & NEW YORK

Copyright © Macmillan Publishers International Ltd 2014
Published in the United States by Kingfisher,
175 Fifth Ave., New York, NY 10010
Kingfisher is an imprint of Macmillan Children's Books, London.
All rights reserved.

Distributed in the U.S. and Canada by Macmillan,
175 Fifth Ave., New York, NY 10010

Library of Congress Cataloging-in-Publication data
has been applied for.

Series editor: Thea Feldman
Literacy consultant: Ellie Costa, Bank Street School for Children, New York
Dinosaur consultant: David Burnie
Illustrations by: Sebastian Quigley, Linden Artists

ISBN: 978-0-7534-7136-4 (HB)
ISBN: 978-0-7534-7137-1 (PB)

Kingfisher books are available for special promotions
and premiums. For details contact: Special Markets
Department, Macmillan, 175 Fifth Ave.,
New York, NY 10010.

For more information, please visit
www.kingfisherbooks.com

Printed in China
9 8 7 6 5
5TR/0818/WKT/UG/105MA

Picture credits
The Publisher would like to thank the following for permission to reproduce their
material. Every care has been taken to trace copyright holders.
Top = t; Bottom = b; Center = c; Left = l; Right = r
Pages 10t Shutterstock/Computer Earth; 10b Shutterstock/Karel Gallas; 11t Shutterstock/
Bull's-Eye Arts; 11b Shutterstock/Heiko Kiera; 28 Science Photo Library/John Mitchell;
29 Shutterstock/joingate; 30–31 Alamy/© David R. Frazier Photolibrary, Inc.

This is a big, fierce **dinosaur**!

It is called Tyrannosaurus
(Tie-RAN-uh-SORE-us).

Tyrannosaurus lived
millions of years ago.

That is a very long
time ago.

There were no people yet.

Let's go back in time
and take a look at
Tyrannosaurus!

Tyrannosaurus is hungry!

He is looking for food.

What does he eat?

Other dinosaurs!
Tyrannosaurus is a hunter.

The animals he hunts
are called his **prey**.

Triceratops (Try-SER-uh-tops) might become his prey.

So might Edmontosaurus (Ed-MON-tuh-SORE-us).

Here are some
other animals
that live in the
same forest.

Tyrannosaurus does
not eat them.

Tyrannosaurus is big.

He needs a lot of food.

So he hunts big animals.

Look!

Tyrannosaurus runs
after his prey.

He runs on his toes.

His tail sticks out behind him.

The tail helps Tyrannosaurus
keep his balance.

Tyrannosaurus catches up with his prey.

He tries to bite Triceratops.

Triceratops fights back with her sharp horns.

Triceratops gets away!

Tyrannosaurus is still hungry.

He runs
through the
forest again.

Tyrannosaurus meets another
Tyrannosaurus.

The two dinosaurs fight.

Why?

Maybe they do not want
to share the same place
in the forest.

One Tyrannosaurus
sinks his teeth
into the other.

The other Tyrannosaurus
runs away.

The winner smells
something new
in the air.

What is it?

It is an Edmontosaurus
that has died.

Tyrannosaurus gulps down
500 pounds of meat in one bite!
(This is over 220 kilograms.)

Tyrannosaurus had a busy day.

He is full and ready for a nap.

How does he sleep?

He can close his eyes
and sleep standing up!

Sometimes he lies
down on the ground.

Dinosaurs lived millions of years ago.

All the dinosaurs are now **extinct**.

This means they have all died.

How do we know so much about them?

Scientists find dinosaur bones buried in sand.

These old bones are called **fossils**.

Scientists study the fossils.

The biggest Tyrannosaurus was found in the USA.

It is named Sue after the scientist who found it.

You can tell just by looking at Sue that Tyrannosaurus was a big, fierce dinosaur!

Glossary

dinosaur a kind of animal that lived millions of years ago

extinct a kind of animal or plant that no longer exists

fossils parts of dead animals that have turned to stone

prey animals that are hunted and eaten by other animals

scientists people who study science and use it in their work